PHYSICAL SCIENCE

SOLIDS AND LIQUIDS

by Mary Lindeen

NORWOOD**H**OUSE **P**RESS

DEAR CAREGIVER, The *Beginning to Read—Read and Discover Science* books provide young readers the opportunity to learn about scientific concepts while simultaneously building early reading skills. Each title corresponds to three of the key domains within the Next Generation Science Standards (NGSS): physical sciences, life sciences, and earth and space sciences.

The NGSS include standards that are comprised of three dimensions: Crosscutting Concepts, Science and Engineering Practices, and Disciplinary Core Ideas. The texts within the *Read and Discover Science* series focus primarily upon the Disciplinary Core Ideas and Crosscutting Concepts—helping readers view their world through a scientific lens. They pique a young reader's curiosity and encourage them to inquire and explore. The Connecting Concepts section at the back of each book offers resources to continue that exploration. The reinforcement activities at the back of the book support Science and Engineering Practices—to understand how scientists investigate phenomena in that world.

These easy-to-read informational texts make the scientific concepts accessible to young readers and prompt them to consider the role of science in their world. On one hand, these titles can develop background knowledge for exploring new topics. Alternately, they can be used to investigate, explain, and expand the findings of one's own inquiry. As you read with your child, encourage her or him to "observe"—taking notice of the images and information to formulate both questions and responses about what, how, and why something is happening.

Above all, the most important part of the reading experience is to have fun and enjoy it!

Sincerely,

Shannon Cannon

Shannon Cannon, PhD
Literacy Consultant

Norwood House Press
For more information about Norwood House Press please visit our website at www.norwoodhousepress.com or call 866-565-2900.
© 2022 Norwood House Press. Beginning-to-Read™ is a trademark of Norwood House Press. All rights reserved. No part of this book may be reproduced or utilized in any form or by any means without written permission from the publisher.

Editor: Judy Kentor Schmauss   **Designer**: Sara Radka

Photo Credits: Getty Images: 1, 3, 4, 8, 10, 12, 16, 17, 18, 22, 23, 24, 26, 27, 28, 29; Shutterstock: 4, 6, 9, 14, 15, 20, 21, 29

Library of Congress Cataloging-in-Publication Data
Names: Lindeen, Mary, author.
Title: Solids and liquids / by Mary Lindeen.
Description: Chicago : Norwood House Press, [2022] | Series: Beginning-to-read | Audience: Grades K-1 | Summary: "Solids and liquids are matter, which is anything that takes up space. A solid can hold its own shape, but a liquid takes on the shape of its container. Includes science and reading activities and a word list"-- Provided by publisher.
Identifiers: LCCN 2021019795 (print) | LCCN 2021019796 (ebook) | ISBN 9781684508259 (hardcover) | ISBN 9781684046577 (paperback) | ISBN 9781684046638 (epub)
Subjects: LCSH: Matter--Juvenile literature.
Classification: LCC QC173.36 .L57 2022 (print) | LCC QC173.36 (ebook) | DDC 530.4--dc23
LC record available at https://lccn.loc.gov/2021019795
LC ebook record available at https://lccn.loc.gov/2021019796

Library ISBN: 978-1-68450-825-9   Paperback ISBN: 978-1-68404-657-7

Are you hungry?

How about a bowl of solids with some liquid?

Cereal and bananas are solids.
Milk is a liquid.

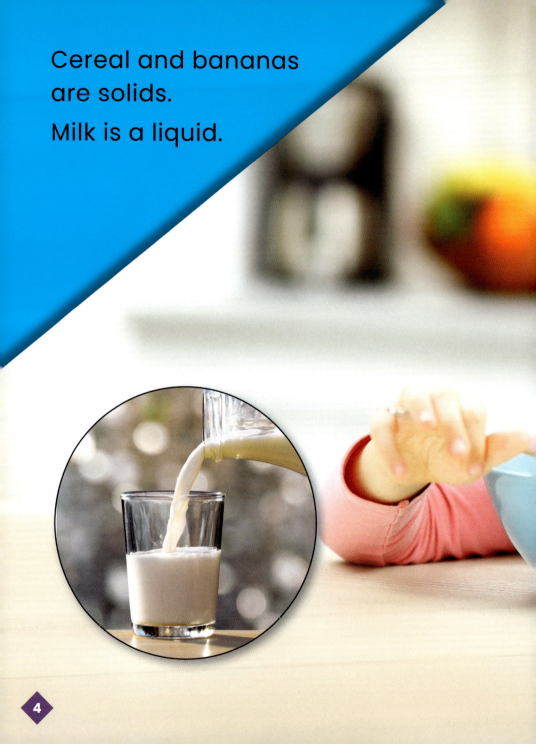

Solids and liquids are both matter.

Did You Know?

Matter is anything that takes up space and has weight.

Everything you can see is made of matter.

Matter can also be things you can't see, like air.

Air takes up space inside this balloon.

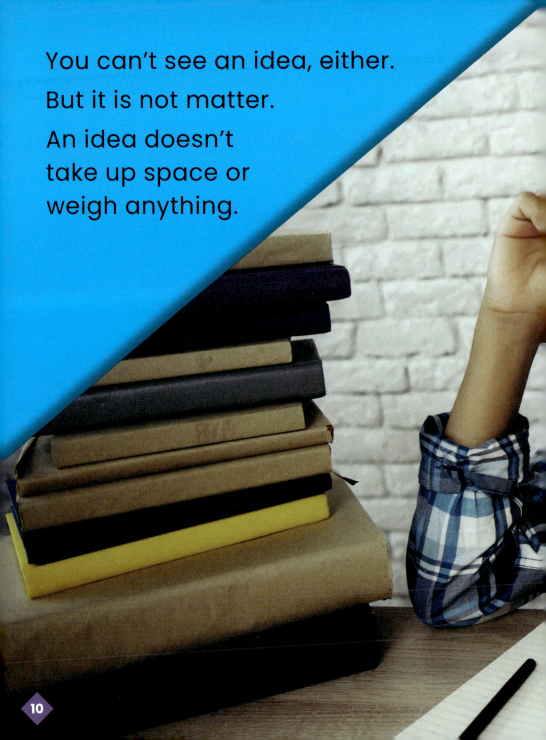

You can't see an idea, either. But it is not matter. An idea doesn't take up space or weigh anything.

A song is not matter, either. But the person who sings it is!

A solid is matter that can hold its own shape.

All of these are solids.

A liquid is matter that cannot hold its own shape.

Did You Know?

Slime is a liquid. It does not hold its own shape.

All of these bottles hold liquids.

A liquid takes the shape of its container.

You can change the shape of a liquid by changing its container.

Solids and liquids are everywhere. They are inside.

They are outside.

They are even in your body!
Teeth and bones are solids.

Tears and blood are liquids.

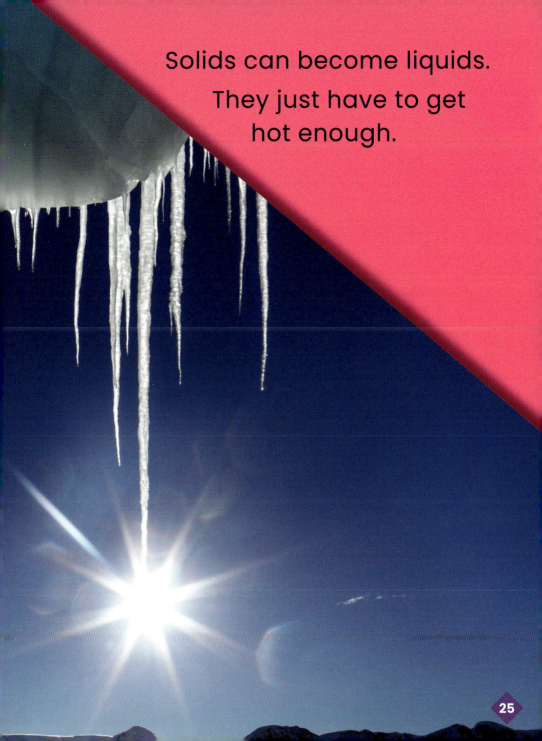

Solids can become liquids. They just have to get hot enough.

Liquids can become solids.

They just have to get cool enough.

Sometimes they have to get very cool!

Solids

Liquids

...READING REINFORCEMENT...

CONNECTING CONCEPTS

UNDERSTANDING SCIENCE CONCEPTS

To check your child's understanding of the information in this book, recreate the following graphic organizer on a sheet of paper. Help your child complete the organizer by identifying the differences between solids and liquids and giving examples of each:

SOLIDS	LIQUIDS

SCIENCE IN THE REAL WORLD

Have your child peel the wrappers off of broken crayons. Put them in a muffin tin and then into a 300° oven for ten minutes. Have your children explain what happened to the crayons. Let them cool and harden and ask your child again what happened.

SCIENCE AND ACADEMIC LANGUAGE

Make sure your child understands the meaning of the following words:

solids   **liquids**   **matter**   **space**   **weigh**   **container**

Have him or her use the words in a sentence.

FLUENCY

Help your child practice fluency by using one or more of the following activities:

1. Reread the book to your child at least two times while he or she uses a finger to track each word as it is read.
2. Read a line of the book, then reread it as your child reads along with you.
3. Ask your child to go back through the book and read the words he or she knows.
4. Have your child practice reading the book several times to improve accuracy, rate, and expression.

FOR FURTHER INFORMATION

Books:

Adler, David A. *Solids, Liquids, Gases, and Plasma*. New York, NY: Holiday House, 2019.

Crane, Cody. *Matter*. New York, NY: Children's Press, 2019.

Diehn, Andi. *Matter: Physical Science for Kids*. White River Junction, VT: Nomad Press, 2018.

Websites:

Homeschool Pop: Solids and Liquids for Kids
https://www.youtube.com/watch?v=nbfIoBQnpK8

PBS Kids: Ready, Jet, Go! States of Matter
https://pbskids.org/video/ready-jet-go/3014321360

Smile and Learn: States of Matter for Kids
https://www.youtube.com/watch?v=JQ4WduVp9k4

Word List

Solids and Liquids uses the 88 words listed below. *High-frequency* words are those words that are used most often in the English language. They are sometimes referred to as sight words because children need to learn to recognize them automatically when they read. *Content* words are any words specific to a particular topic. Regular practice reading these words will enhance your child's ability to read with greater fluency and comprehension.

HIGH-FREQUENCY WORDS

a	but	is	see	up
about	by	it	some	very
air	can	its	take(s)	who
all	does	just	that	with
also	even	like	the	you
an	get	made	these	your
and	has	not	they	
are	have	of	things	
be	how	or	this	
both	in	own	to	

CONTENT WORDS

anything	cannot	enough	matter	song
balloon	can't	everything	milk	space
bananas	cereal	everywhere	outside	tears
become	change	hold	person	teeth
blood	changing	hot	shape	weigh
body	container	hungry	sings	weight
bones	cool	idea	slime	
bottles	doesn't	inside	solid(s)	
bowl	either	liquid(s)	sometimes	

About the Author

Mary Lindeen is a writer, editor, parent, and former elementary school teacher. She has written more than 100 books for children and edited many more. She specializes in early literacy instruction and books for young readers, especially nonfiction.

About the Advisor

Dr. Shannon Cannon is an elementary school teacher in Sacramento, California. She has served as a teacher educator in the School of Education at UC Davis, where she also earned her PhD in Language, Literacy, and Culture. As a member of the clinical faculty, she supervised pre-service teachers and taught elementary methods courses in reading, effective teaching, and teacher action research.